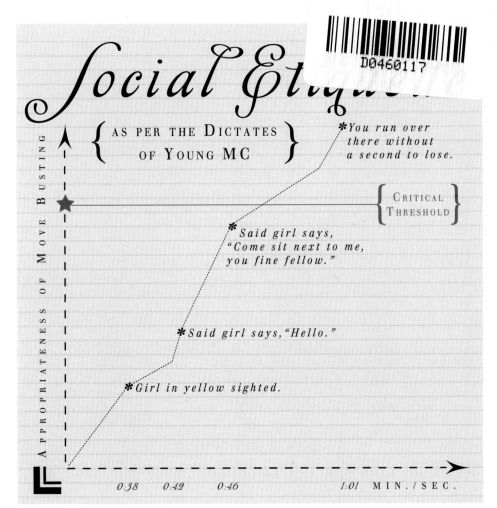

Social Etiquette

{ AS PER THE DICTATES OF YOUNG MC }

APPROPRIATENESS OF MOVE BUSTING

{ CRITICAL THRESHOLD }

* You run over there without a second to lose.

* Said girl says, "Come sit next to me, you fine fellow."

* Said girl says, "Hello."

* Girl in yellow sighted.

0:38   0:42   0:46   1:01   MIN./SEC.

DECISION VS. THE AMOUNT OF ENSUING TROUBLE

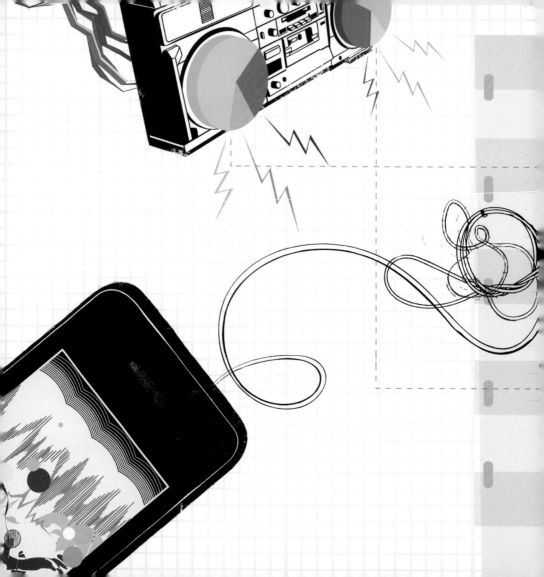

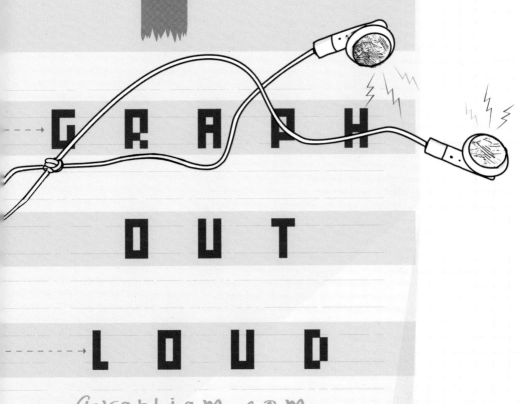

GRAPH

OUT

LOUD

Graphjam.com

GOTHAM BOOKS

GOTHAM BOOKS
Published by Penguin Group (USA) Inc.
375 Hudson Street, New York, New York 10014, U.S.A.

Penguin Group (Canada), 90 Eglinton Avenue East, Suite 700, Toronto, Ontario M4P 2Y3, Canada (a division of Pearson Penguin Canada Inc.); Penguin Books Ltd, 80 Strand, London WC2R 0RL, England; Penguin Ireland, 25 St Stephen's Green, Dublin 2, Ireland (a division of Penguin Books Ltd); Penguin Group (Australia), 250 Camberwell Road, Camberwell, Victoria 3124, Australia (a division of Pearson Australia Group Pty Ltd); Penguin Books India Pvt Ltd, 11 Community Centre, Panchsheel Park, New Delhi - 110 017, India; Penguin Group (NZ), 67 Apollo Drive, Rosedale, North Shore 0632, New Zealand (a division of Pearson New Zealand Ltd); Penguin Books (South Africa) (Pty) Ltd, 24 Sturdee Avenue, Rosebank, Johannesburg 2196, South Africa

Penguin Books Ltd, Registered Offices: 80 Strand, London WC2R 0RL, England

Published by Gotham Books, a member of Penguin Group (USA) Inc.

First printing, October 2009
10 9 8 7 6 5 4 3 2 1

Graph out loud / GraphJam.com.
p. cm.
ISBN 978-1-59240-487-2 (pbk.)
1. Popular culture--Humor. 2. Charts, diagrams, etc.--Humor. 3. Web
sites--Humor. I. GraphJam.com.
PN6231.P635G73 2009
818'.602--dc22

Gotham Books and the skyscraper logo are trademarks of Penguin Group (USA) Inc.

ISBN 978-1-592-40487-2

Printed in the United States of America
Book illustration and design by Ben Gibson

AN INVESTIGATION INTO ERRATIC PRICE MOVEMENTS OF FROZEN CONCENTRATED ORANGE JUICE FUTURES (FCOJ) ON 14 APRIL 1983

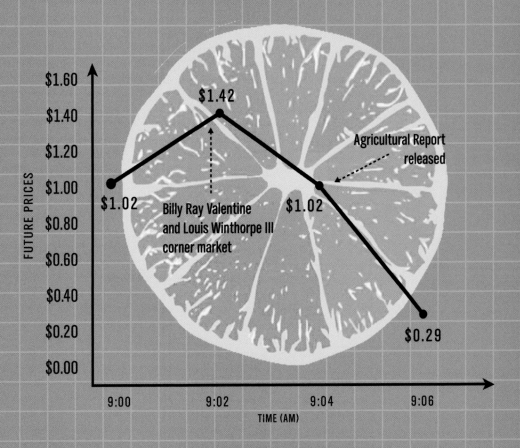

FUTURE PRICES

$1.60
$1.40
$1.20
$1.00
$0.80
$0.60
$0.40
$0.20
$0.00

$1.42

$1.02

Billy Ray Valentine
and Louis Winthorpe III
corner market

Agricultural Report
released

$1.02

$0.29

9:00   9:02   9:04   9:06

TIME (AM)

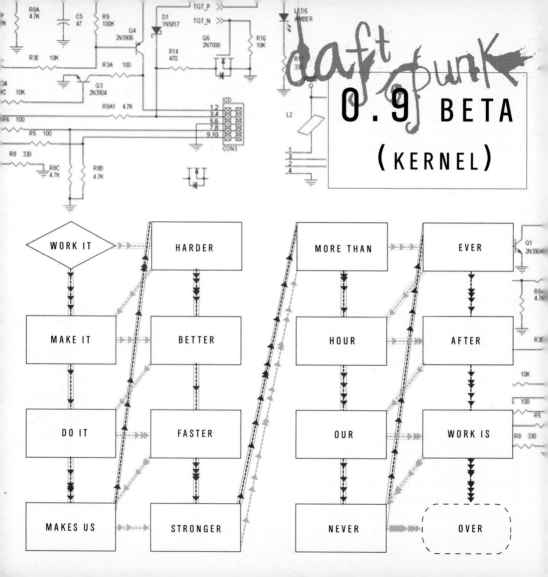

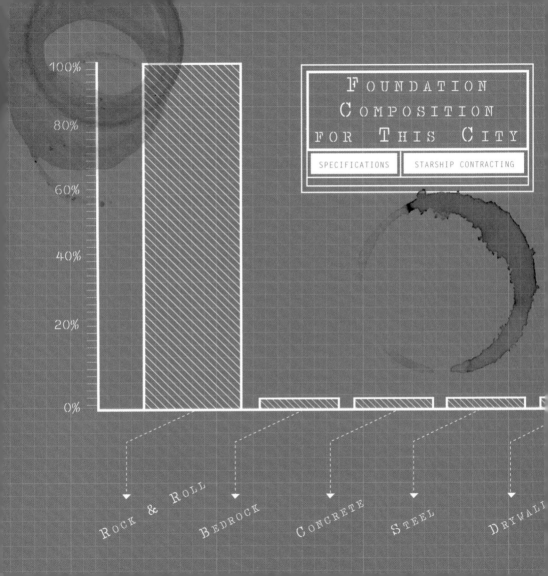

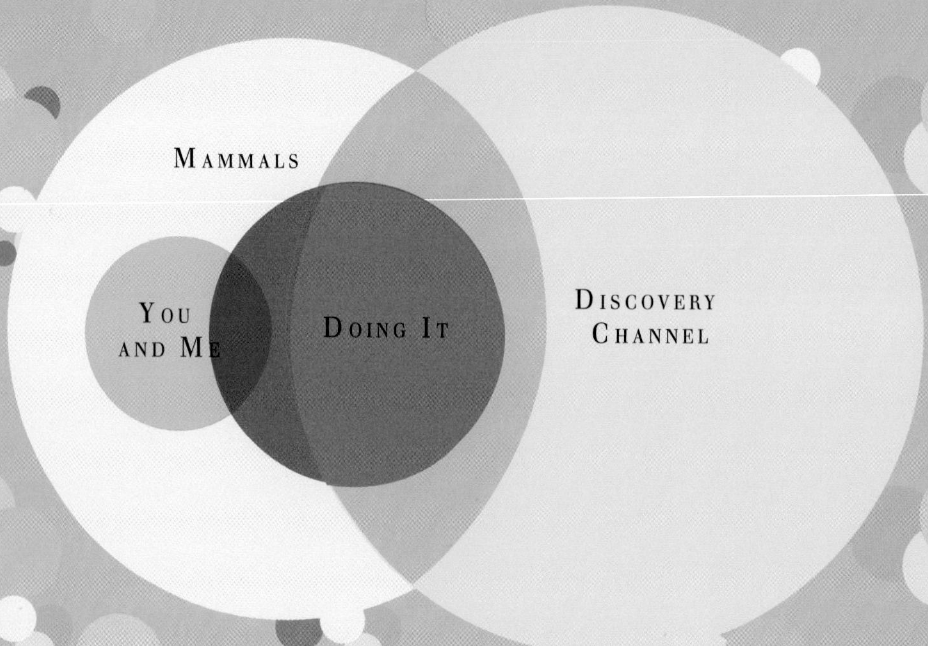

MAMMALS

YOU
AND ME

DOING IT

DISCOVERY
CHANNEL

{ *INSPIRATION* }

A
PROBLEM
COMES
ALONG

GO
FORWARD

◀ ·YES· · · · · ·

MOVE
AHEAD

IS IT
IN SHAPE?

NO

IS IT
TOO LATE?

· · NO ▶

WHIP IT!

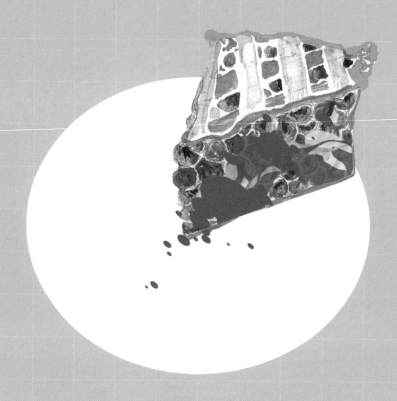

AMOUNT OF PIE EATEN ● AMOUNT OF PIE NOT YET EATEN

Items needed for a 106-mile drive to Chicago at night

{ per the mission director* }

Packs of cigarettes — 1

Tanks of gas — 0.5

Pairs of sunglasses — 2

0   0.5   1   2   2.5

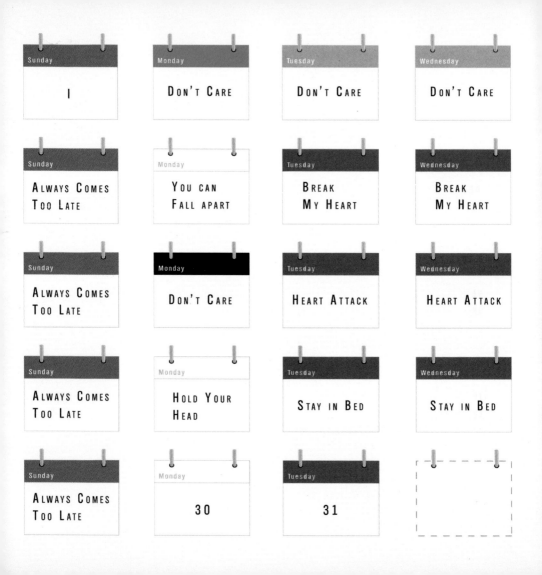

Thursday

DON'T CARE
ABOUT YOU

Saturday

WAIT

Thursday

DOESN'T
EVEN START

Saturday

WAIT

Friday

I'M IN

Thursday

NEVER
LOOKING BACK

Saturday

WAIT

Thursday

WATCH THE
WALLS INSTEAD

Saturday

WAIT

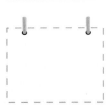

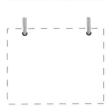

Attn: Mrs. Robinson

AMOUNT OF JESUS'S LOVE YOU WILL KNOW   ACTUAL AMOUNT OF JESUS'S LOVE

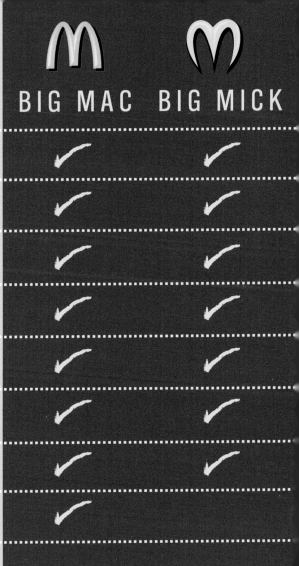

INGREDIENT	BIG MAC	BIG MICK
TWO ALL-BEEF PATTIES	✓	✓
SPECIAL SAUCE	✓	✓
LETTUCE	✓	✓
CHEESE	✓	✓
PICKLE	✓	✓
ONION	✓	✓
BUN	✓	✓
SESAME SEEDS	✓	

PROBLEMS

MONEY

RELATIONSHIP
BETWEEN
MONEY
AND PROBLEMS

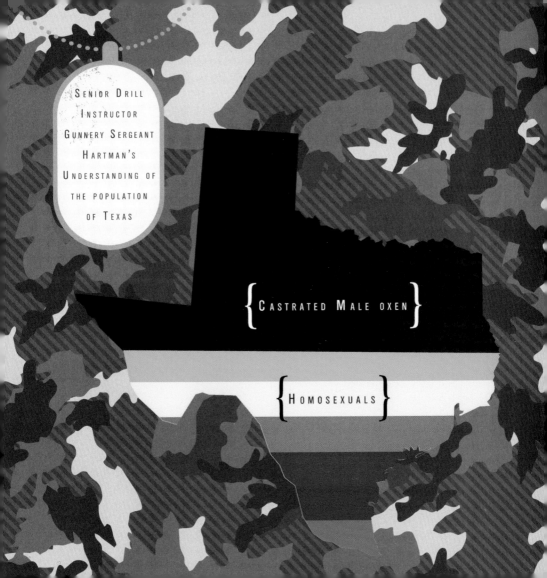

SENIOR DRILL INSTRUCTOR GUNNERY SERGEANT HARTMAN'S UNDERSTANDING OF THE POPULATION OF TEXAS

{ CASTRATED MALE OXEN }

{ HOMOSEXUALS }

RELATIVE AWESOMENESS OF LEAD SINGERS

AWESOME }

AS VISUALIZED IN TERMS OF SCALE,
LOCOMOTION, COLOR, CHAOS.

LAME }

SAMMY HAGAR

DAVID LEE ROTH

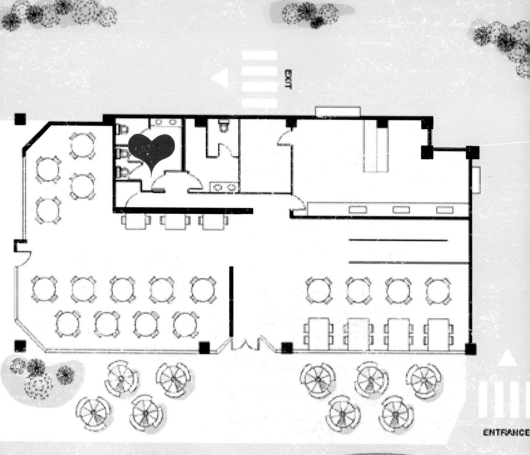

EXIT

ENTRANCE

{ PLACES HUMPTY HAS GOTTEN BUSY }

BURGER
KING

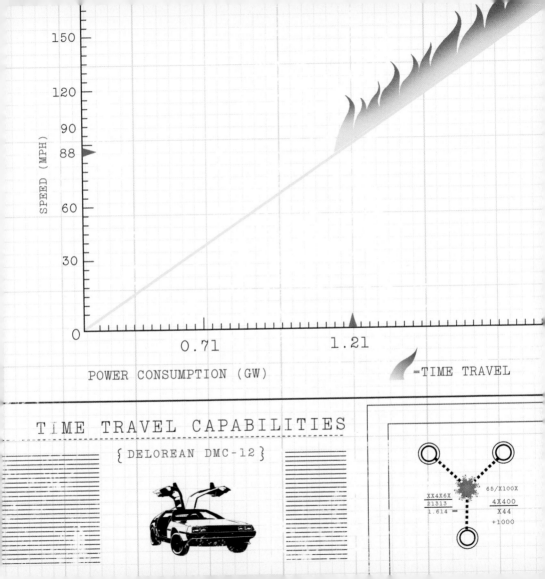

SPEED (MPH)

150

120

90
88

60

30

0

0.71   1.21

POWER CONSUMPTION (GW)

▲ =TIME TRAVEL

TIME TRAVEL CAPABILITIES

{ DELOREAN DMC-12 }

XX4X6X
—————
21313
—————
1.614 =

65/X100X
—————
4X400
—————
X44
+1000

Driving Your
Enemies Before You

Crushing
Your
Enemies

Hearing the
Lamentation of
their Women

Things That are Best in Life

Dream Weaver To-Do List

- [x] Get me through the night
- [x] Reach the morning light
- [x] Cross the highways of fantasy
- [x] Help me forget today's pain
- [x] Fly me away
- [x] (to the bright side of the moon)
- [x] Meet me on the other side

THE GOOD + THE BAD = THE FACTS OF LIFE

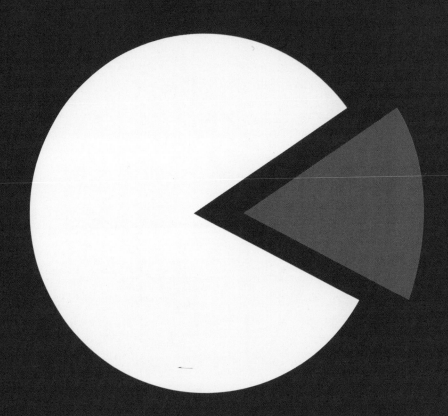

Games Played in the 1980s

Pacman   Trivial Pursuit

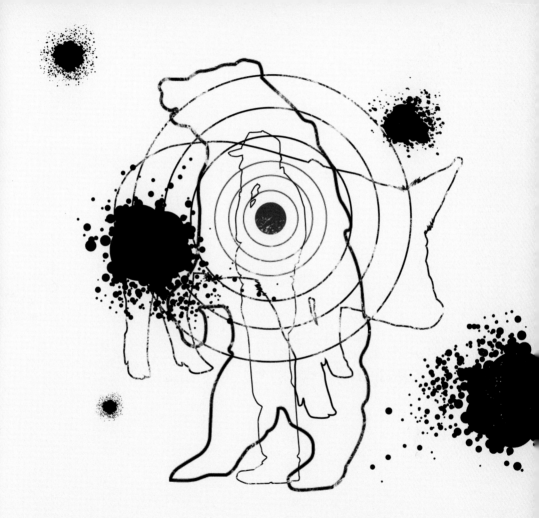

SUPER SERIAL BUSINESS

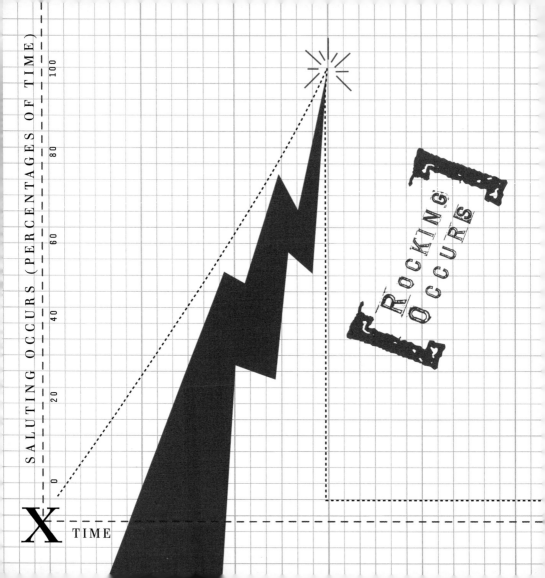

NUMBER OF LAW OFFICERS KILLED BY POPULAR MUSICIANS

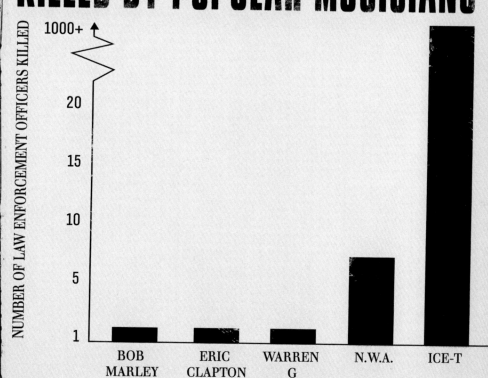

NUMBER OF LAW ENFORCEMENT OFFICERS KILLED

1000+

20

15

10

5

1

BOB MARLEY | ERIC CLAPTON | WARREN G | N.W.A. | ICE-T

SHOCKING NEW EVIDENCE SUPPORTS STUDIES

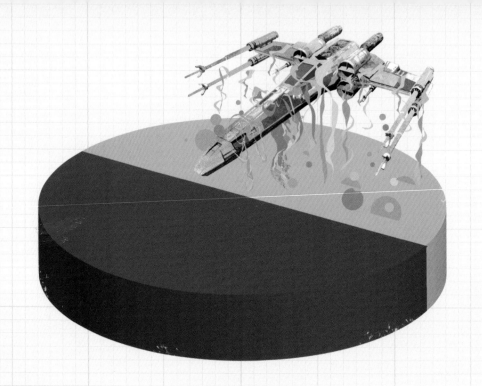

YOUR OPTIONS WHEN LIFTING A LARGE SPACECRAFT OUT OF A SWAMP USING THE FORCE
{ACCORDING TO YODA}

 ● DO ● DO NOT ● TRY

REKALL

INDUSTRIES

FOR THE MEMORY OF A LIFETIME

3084 RADTLE DRIVE SUITE 42 PHILADELPHIA, PA 19102 EARTH

TO: QUAID
FROM: HAUSER

JULY 3RD, 2084

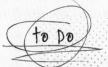
to do

1. Visit Rekall.
2. Get Ass to Mars.
3. Meet with Melina.
4. Infiltrate Mutant Resistance.
5. Meet with Kuato.
6. ~~Erase Mind, revert to Hauser.~~
6. Start Reactor.
7. Free Mars.

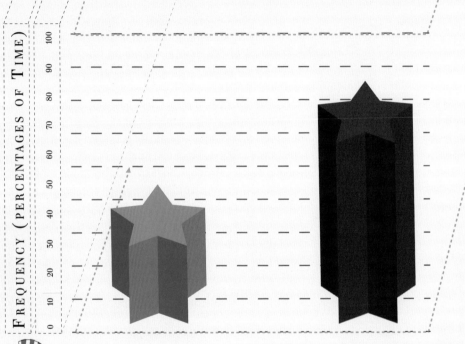

FREQUENCY (PERCENTAGES OF TIME)

100 — 90 — 80 — 70 — 60 — 50 — 40 — 30 — 20 — 10 — 0

 ★ WHAT YOU WANT ←——→ WHAT YOU NEED* ★

<<<<<<<<<<<<<<< NECESSITY >>>>>>>>>>>>>>

PROBABILITY OF GETTING THINGS *IF YOU TRY

R.E.M.'S RECOMMENDED METHOD OF DEPRESSION MANAGEMENT

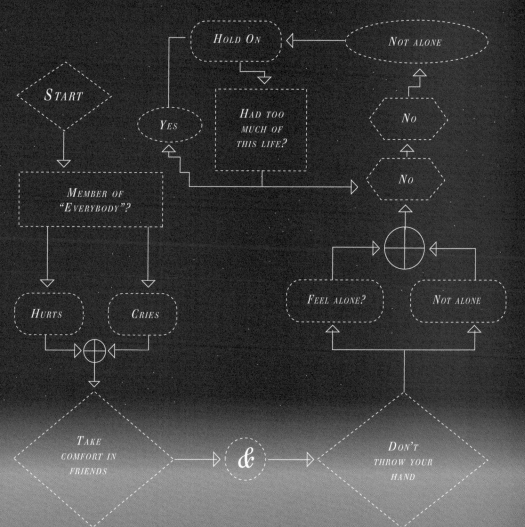

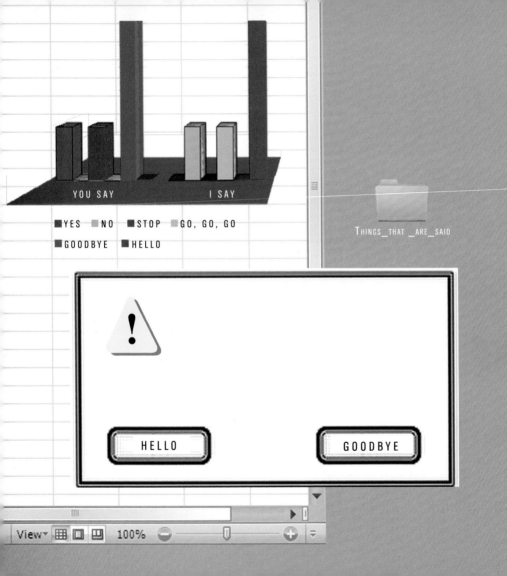

● AMOUNT OF PIE EATEN   ● AMOUNT OF PIE NOT YET EATEN

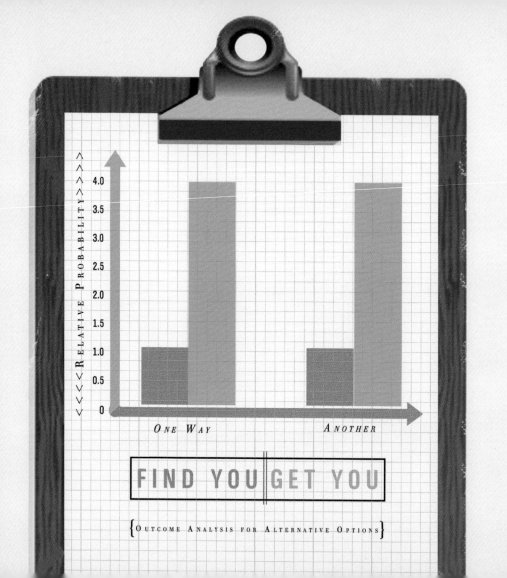

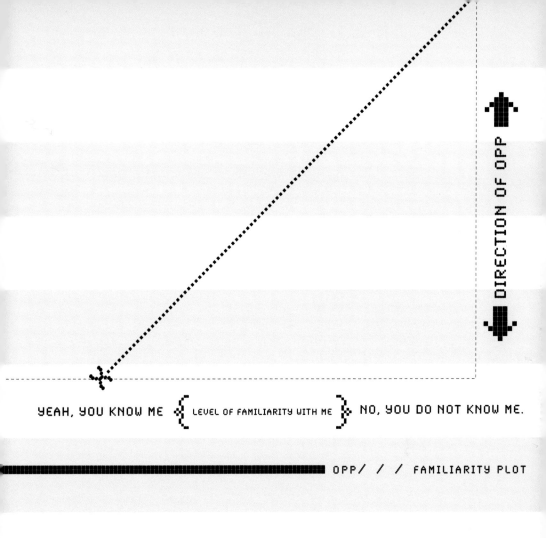

DIRECTION OF OPP

YEAH, YOU KNOW ME ❬ LEVEL OF FAMILIARITY WITH ME ❭ NO, YOU DO NOT KNOW ME.

OPP/ / / FAMILIARITY PLOT

15°	16°	17°	18°	19°	20°	21°
22°	23°	24°	25°	26°	27°	28°
29°	30°	1	2	3	4	5

● 12AM-8AM ROCK & ROLL
● 8AM-8PM PARTY
● 8PM-12AM ROCK & ROLL

| Today | List | Day | Month | ↓ |

15°	16°	17°	18°	19°	20°	21°
22°	23°	24°	25°	26°	27°	28°
29°	30°	1	2	3	4	5

● 12AM-8AM ROCK & ROLL
● 8AM-8PM PARTY
● 8PM-12AM ROCK & ROLL

| Today | List | Day | Month | ↓ |

GENE   PAUL

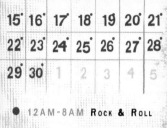

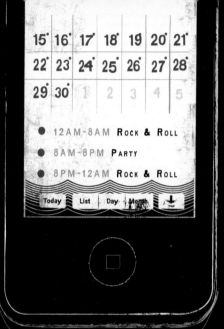

Distribution Of my KnOωLEdgE

What you did
(seasonally)

	Know	Don't know
Last winter		✕
Last spring		✕
Last summer		
Last summer		✕

Maybe I'm...

MY FATHER

MY MOTHER

TOO BOLD

NEVER SATISFIED

TOO DEMANDING

Don't cry

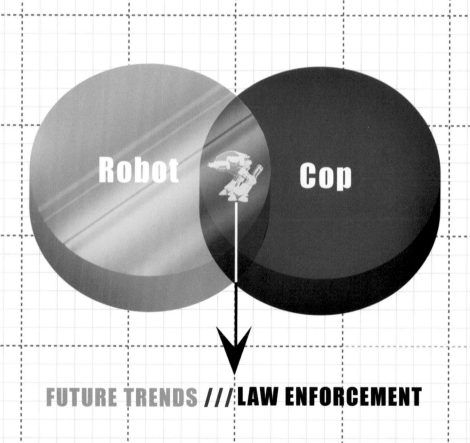

Robot

Cop

FUTURE TRENDS /// LAW ENFORCEMENT

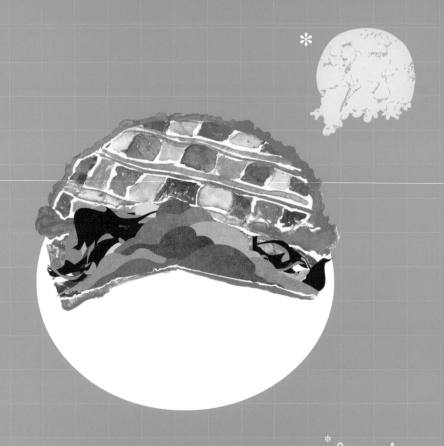

● AMOUNT OF PIE EATEN ● AMOUNT OF PIE NOT YET EATEN

NATURAL DISASTERS
THAT ROCK YOU

1984
★ ★ ★
★ ★ ★

EARTHQUAKE   TYPHOON   HURRICANE

100%
90%
80%
70%
60%
50%
40%
30%
20%
10%
0%

PERCENTAGE OF ROCK

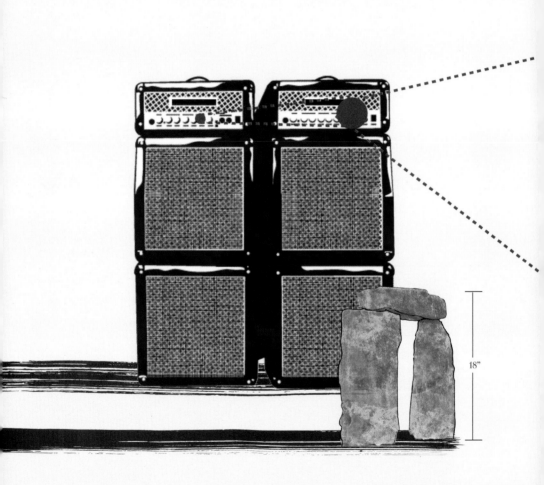

18"

MAXIMUM VOLUME
OF
GUITAR AMPLIFIERS

Fig. 9

Where Karate
Resides

{ As per Mr. Miyagi }

Red =
Karate

0000 HRS 0100 HRS 0200 HRS 0300 HRS 0400 HRS 0500 HRS 0600 HRS 0700 HRS 0800 HRS 0900 HRS 1000 HRS 1100 HRS 1200 HRS 1300 HRS 1400 HRS 1500 HRS 1600 HRS 1700 HRS 1800 HRS 1900 HRS 2000 HRS 2100 HRS 2200 HRS 2300 HRS

Time Spent Wearing Sunglasses (06/16/1983)

You   Me

12-35
000

CHECK NO.

F-14

FUNDS

AMOUNT:

Bringing Cougar in,
breaking the Hard Deck,
violating the
Rules of Engagement

EGOTIABLE

Maverick's Ego

MEMO: Let's buzz the tower, too

WORKS
EVERY TIME
(60%)

OTHER
(40%)

SEX PANTHER COLOGNE
★ ★ ★ ★ ★ EFFECTIVENESS STUDY ★ ★ ★ ★ ★

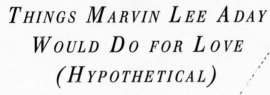

THINGS MARVIN LEE ADAY WOULD DO FOR LOVE (HYPOTHETICAL)

c. 1993

GET YOU RIGHT OUT OF THIS GODFORSAKEN TOWN

MAKE IT ALL A LITTLE LESS COLD

HOSE YOU DOWN WITH HOLY WATER (IF YOU GET TOO HOT)

ANYTHING {100%}

THAT {0%}

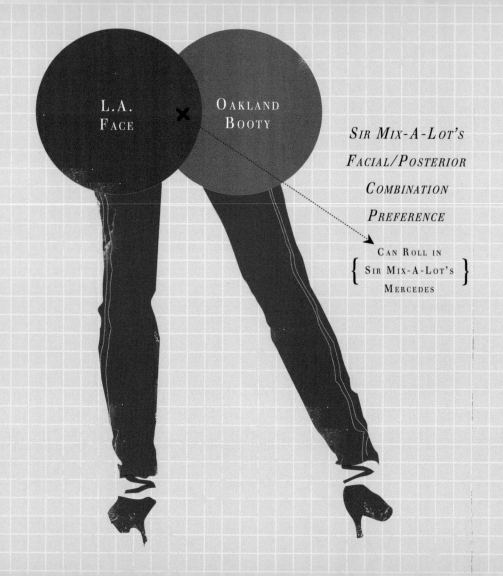

L.A. FACE × OAKLAND BOOTY

SIR MIX-A-LOT'S FACIAL/POSTERIOR COMBINATION PREFERENCE

CAN ROLL IN { SIR MIX-A-LOT'S } MERCEDES

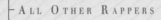
ALL OTHER RAPPERS

N.W.A.

THANKS GOTTEN

INVOLVEMENT IN STARTING
THIS GANGSTA SHIT

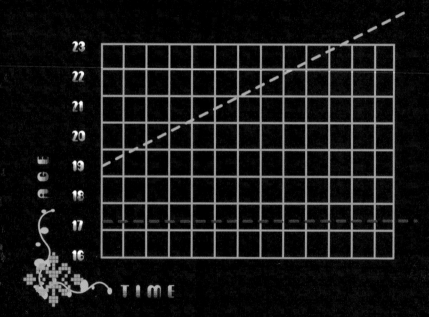

The Thing I Like about High School Girls

AGE
23
22
21
20
19
18
17
16

TIME

Wooderson   High School Girls

SUNDAY	MONDAY	TUESDAY	WEDNESDAY	
1	2	3	4	

DAYS ALLOTTED FOR LOVING YOU {PER WEEK}

5 6 7

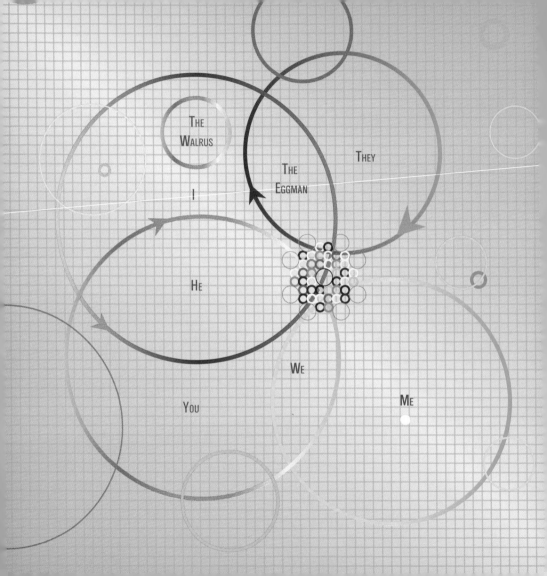

INVENTION

A

B
C
D

(A) Perspiration (B) Electricity (C) Evaporation (D) Butterscotch Ripple

93%   6%   4%   2%

THE KNIVINESS OF
A SMALL SAMPLING OF KNIVES

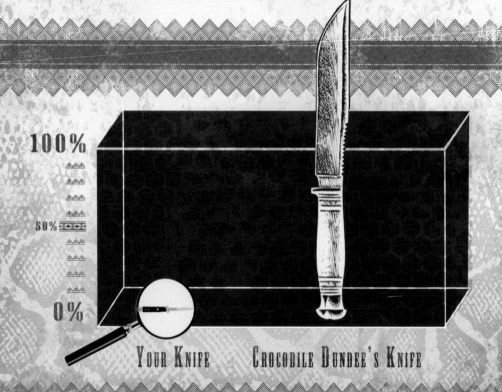

100%

50%

0%

YOUR KNIFE   CROCODILE DUNDEE'S KNIFE

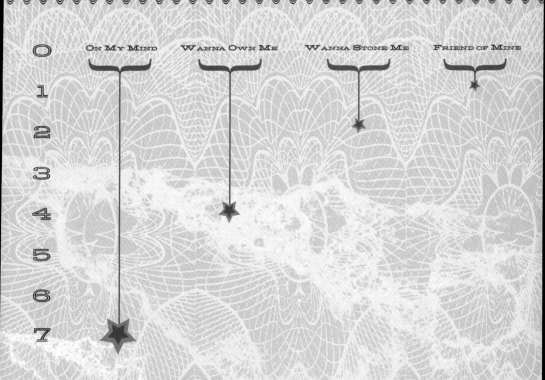

ON MY MIND   WANNA OWN ME   WANNA STONE ME   FRIEND OF MINE

0
1
2
3
4
5
6
7

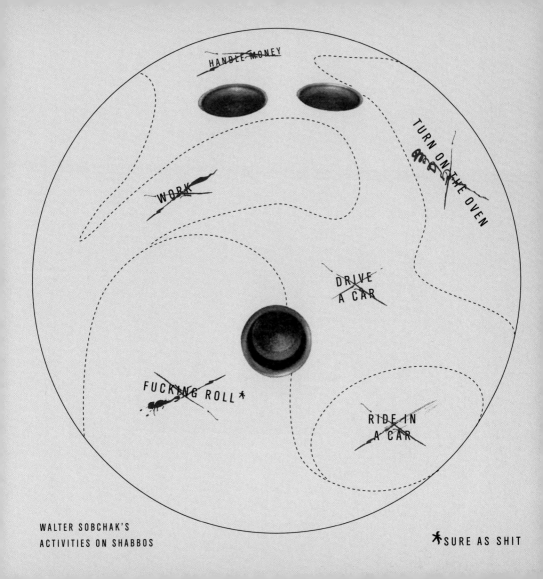

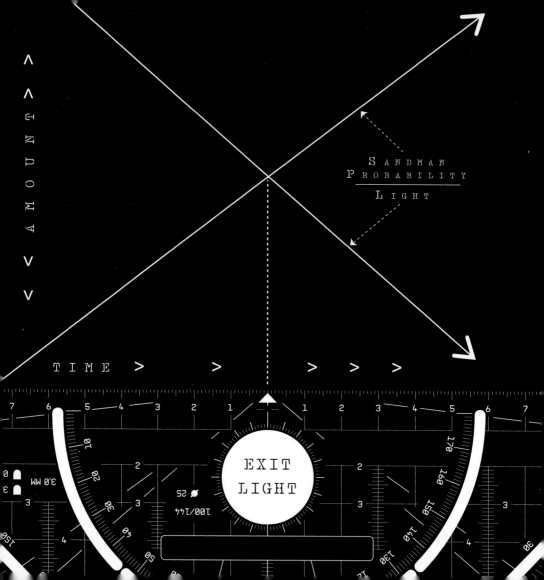

AMY WINEHOUSE'S POSSIBLE RESPONSES TO REHAB

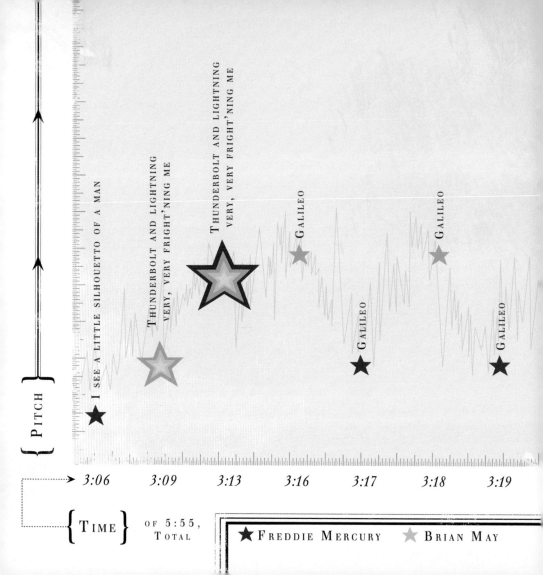

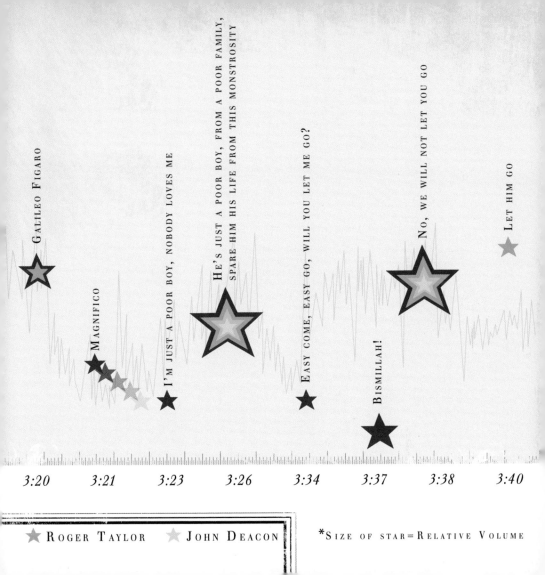

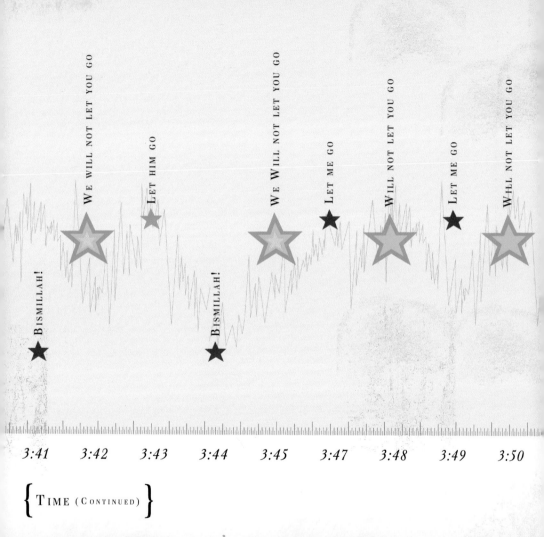

WE WILL NOT LET YOU GO

LET HIM GO

WE WILL NOT LET YOU GO

LET ME GO

WILL NOT LET YOU GO

LET ME GO

WILL NOT LET YOU GO

BISMILLAH!

BISMILLAH!

3:41   3:42   3:43   3:44   3:45   3:47   3:48   3:49   3:50

{ TIME (CONTINUED) }

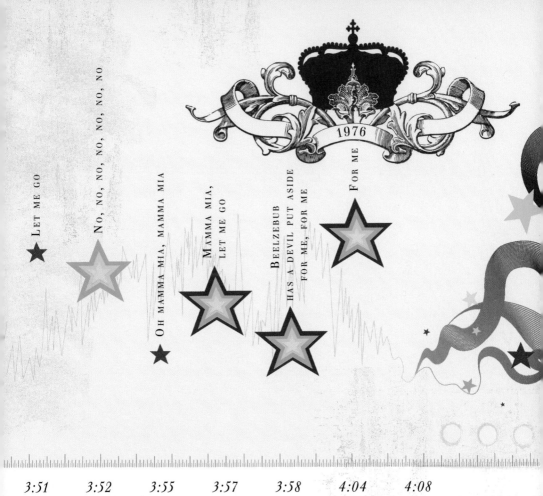

LET ME GO

NO, NO, NO, NO, NO, NO

OH MAMMA MIA, MAMMA MIA

MAMMA MIA, LET ME GO

BEELZEBUB HAS A DEVIL PUT ASIDE FOR ME, FOR ME

FOR ME

1976

3:51 3:52 3:55 3:57 3:58 4:04 4:08

A REAS OF DEPRESSION IN PONIES { PER THE DICTATES OF DAVID BERMAN }

★ BANDITS IN THE CAPITAL   ★ LIMITED CIVILIAN UNREST   ★ COWS IN THE BALLROOM

★ CHICKENS IN THE FARMER'S CORVETTE   ★ UNREASONABLY SHARP GRASS IN THE PASTURE

● AMOUNT OF PIE EATEN   ◐ AMOUNT OF PIE NOT YET EATEN

$$\frac{(\text{WANT YOU}) + (\text{NEED YOU})}{(\text{WANT YOU}) + (\text{NEED YOU}) + (\text{LOVE YOU})} = \frac{2}{3} = (\text{ain't bad})$$

$\dfrac{\partial^2 u}{\partial t^2}$

$+ \partial$

$) x$

$u -$

$(t) dt = \dfrac{x(t)}{dt^n} = ((\omega)$

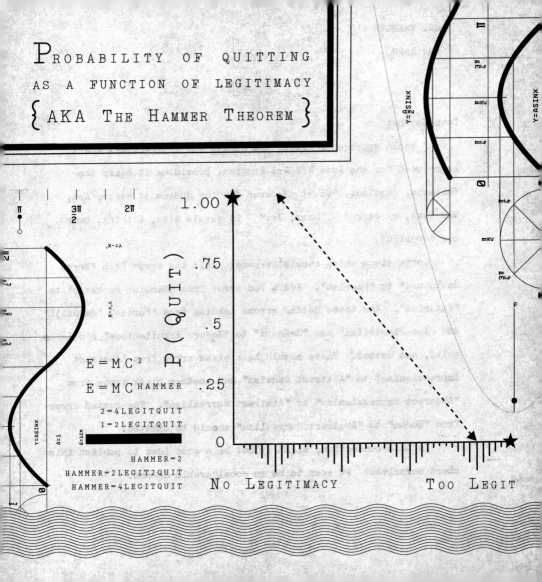

{ COUNTRIES THAT MAY CRY FOR ME }

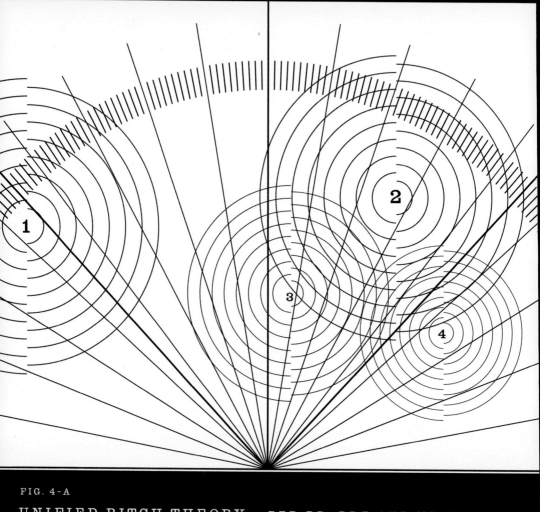

FIG. 4-A

UNIFIED BITCH THEORY ‹‹PER DR. DRE AND MR. DOGG››

(1) SHIT   (2) BITCHES   (3) HOES   (4) TRICKS

The Black Night

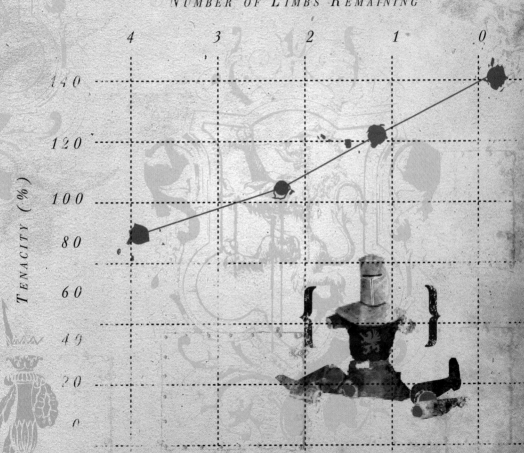

Number of Limbs Remaining

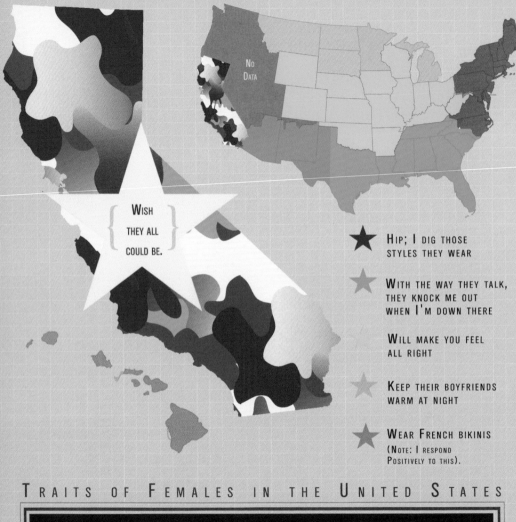

WISH
{ THEY ALL }
COULD BE.

★ HIP; I DIG THOSE
STYLES THEY WEAR

★ WITH THE WAY THEY TALK,
THEY KNOCK ME OUT
WHEN I'M DOWN THERE

★ WILL MAKE YOU FEEL
ALL RIGHT

★ KEEP THEIR BOYFRIENDS
WARM AT NIGHT

★ WEAR FRENCH BIKINIS
(NOTE: I RESPOND
POSITIVELY TO THIS).

No
Data

TRAITS OF FEMALES IN THE UNITED STATES

PRIMARY RESEARCH CONDUCTED BY B. WILSON (1965) AND D. L. ROTH (1985)

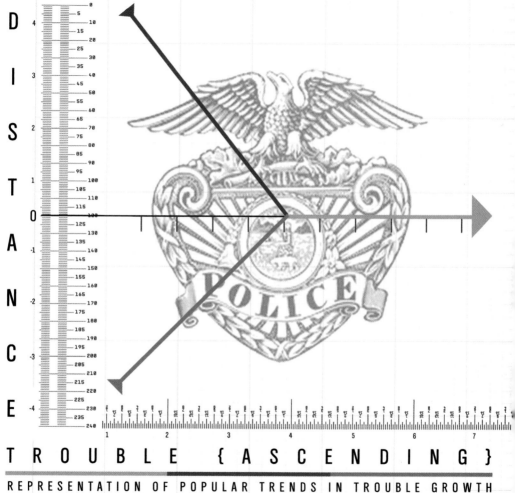

DISTANCE

TROUBLE {ASCENDING}

REPRESENTATION OF POPULAR TRENDS IN TROUBLE GROWTH

LONG BEACH COMPTON

COMPOSITION
OF

RUN
DMC

STATE-BY-STATE DISTRIBUTION
OF THINGS IMPORTANT TO GEORGE STRAIT

EX'S ✶ HATS

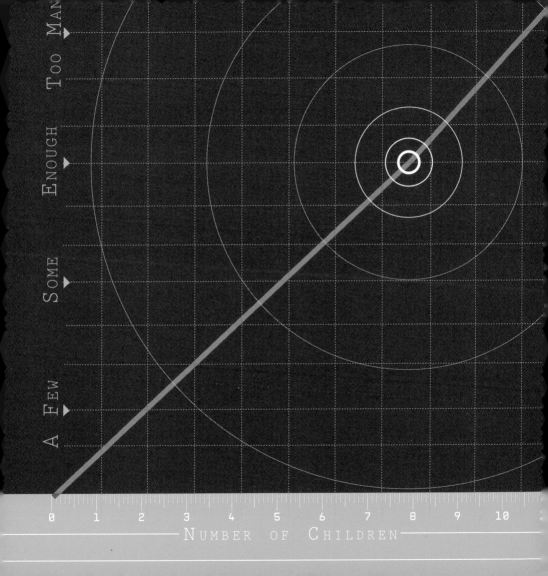

TOO MANY ▸

ENOUGH ▸

SOME ▸

A FEW ▸

0   1   2   3   4   5   6   7   8   9   10

NUMBER OF CHILDREN

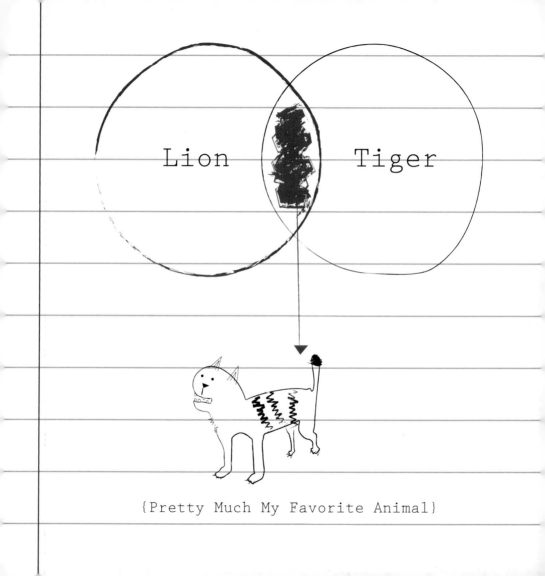

Lion   Tiger

{Pretty Much My Favorite Animal}

In tune ---->   <----*In tune*

ALL THAT YOU...	* *LOVE*	* *BUY*	* *DO*
* *TOUCH*	* *HATE*	* *BEG*	* *SAY*
* *SEE*	* *DISTRUST*	* *BORROW*	* *EAT*
* *TASTE*	* *SAVE*	* *STEAL*	* *MEET*
* *FEEL*	* *GIVE*	* *CREATE*	* *SIGHT*
	* *DEAL*	* *DESTROY*	* *FIGHT*

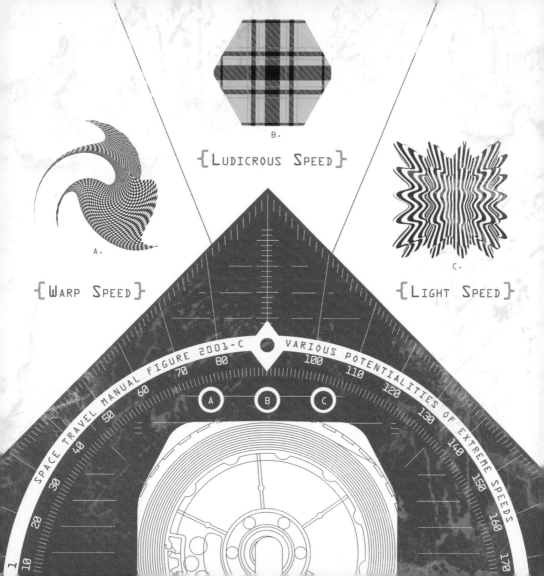

B.

{ LUDICROUS SPEED }

A.

{ WARP SPEED }

C.

{ LIGHT SPEED }

SPACE TRAVEL MANUAL FIGURE 2001-C VARIOUS POTENTIALITIES OF EXTREME SPEEDS

1 10 20 30 40 50 60 70 80 100 110 120 130 140 150 160 170

A B C

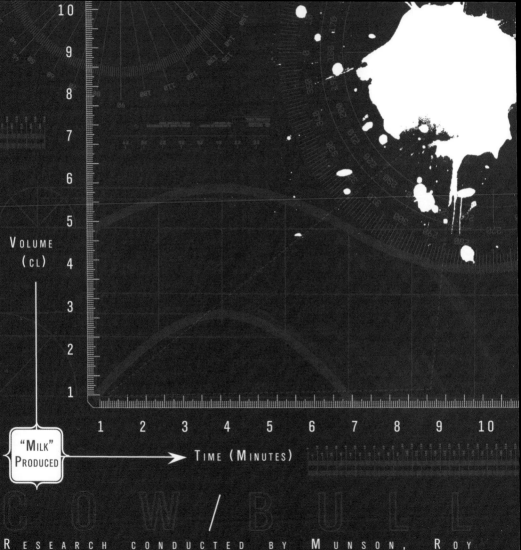

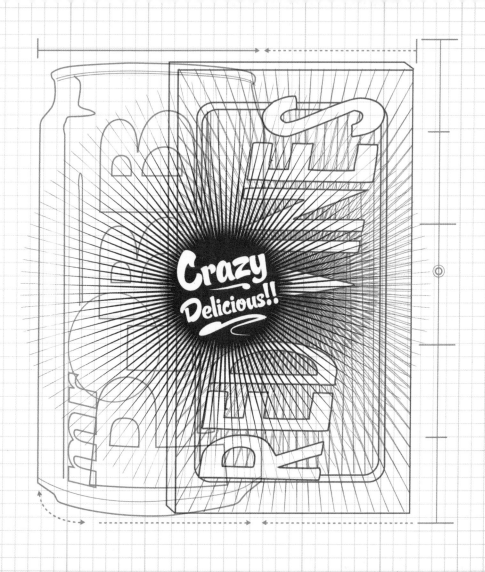

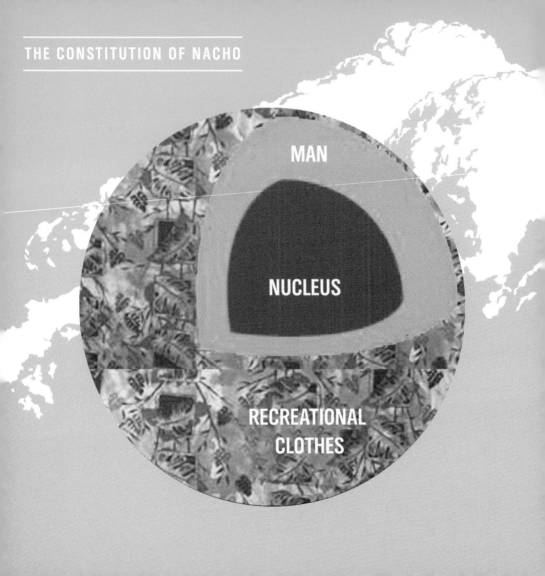

THE CONSTITUTION OF NACHO

MAN

NUCLEUS

RECREATIONAL
CLOTHES

Rick Astley

5/21 1985

	NEVER GONNA	GONNA
Know the Rules	☐	☑
Full Commitment	☐	☑
Make You Understand	☐	☑
Give You Up	☑	☐
Let You Down	☑	☐
Run Around and Desert You	☑	☐
Make You Cry	☑	☐
Say Good-bye	☑	☐
Tell a Lie and Hurt You	☑	☐

(1) IF CIRCUMFERENCE OF CHEST IS GREATER THAN OR EQUAL TO 36 INCHES

AND IF CIRCUMFERENCE OF WAIST IS LESS THAN OR EQUAL TO 24 INCHES (3)

(2) AND IF CIRCUMFERENCE OF HIPS IS GREATER THAN OR EQUAL TO 36 INCHES

AND IF HEIGHT (4) IS LESS THAN OR EQUAL TO 5 FEET 3 INCHES

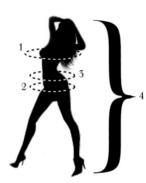

THEN

BABY GOT BACK

Snoop Doggy Dogg's Schedule for the week of June 1st, 1992

Task Name	Start	Finish	June 1992						
			1	2	3	4	5	6	7
Come up with funky ass shit	6/1/1992	6/7/1992	▓	▓	▓	▓	▓	▓	▓
Kick a little something for the Gs	6/5/1992	6/5/1992					▓		
Make a few ends	6/5/1992	6/6/1992					▓	▓	
Party	6/5/1992	6 AM					▓		
Momma comes home	6/7/1992	6/7/1992							▓

1.   2.

3.

4.

5.

NOTHING
AND YOU'LL LIKE IT

6.

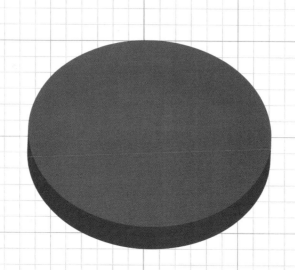

● THE GAME ● THE PLAYER

Things to Hate

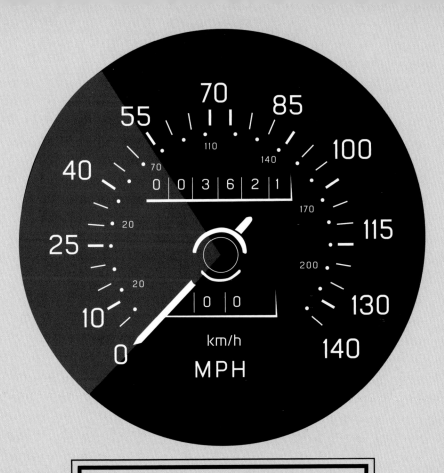

P · R · O · B · L · E · M · S

↓

RAP PATROL · GAT PATROL · FOES · MY CASKET'S CLOSED · RAP CRITICS · MONEY CASH HOES · THE HOOD, STUPID · FACTS · HOLES IN YA ZAPATOS · CELEBRATING · WHOLE ASS HOLE · RADIO · RAP MAGS · MY BLACK ASS · ADVERTIS-ERS · MORE CASH · ADS · FUCKERS · INTELLIGENCE JAY-Z · RAGS · RICHES · NIGGAZ · '94 · MY TRUNK · MY REAR VIEW MIRROR · THE MUTHERFUCKIN' · TWO CHOICES (2) · THE CAR · PEDAL · THE FLOOR · HIGHWAY CHASE · JAY · A FEW DOLLARS · THE CASE · THE SIDE OF THE ROAD · I'M YOUNG · I'M BLACK · MY HAT · A MIND READER · ARREST FIFTY-FIVE · A FIFTY-FO' · LICENSE · REGISTRATION · A WEAPON · MY PAPERS · GLOVE COMPARTMENT · TRUNK RIGHTS · WARRANT · A TACK · LAWYER · SOMEBODY IMPOR-TANT · THE BAR · MY SHIT · THE CANINE · A NIGGA STRONG ARM · A HO · A PUSSY · GODDAMN SENSE · ME THE LORD PRAY · HIM · SOME FOOLS · TO PERFORM · THE TYPE · A MOTORBIKE · A GRAPE · A FRUIT FIGHT · CLAPPIN' · HI BOYS (3) · YAPPIN' · TRAPPED · THE KIT-KAT AGAIN · THE SYSTEM · THE RIFF RAFF AGAIN · FRIENDS · THE FLOOR · PAPARAZZIS · CAMERAS · D.A. · NIGGA SHAFT · HALF-A-MIL FOR BAIL · I'M AFRICAN · THIS FOOL · HARASSIN' THEM · TRYING TO PLAY THE BOY · SACCHARIN · NUTTIN' SWEET · I HOLD MY GUN · YOU'RE CRAZY · RICK · YOUR BOY ▬

A BITCH

Directions:Shake

% POSITIVE OLFACTORY RESPONSE TO NAPALM

0% 20% 40% 60% 80% 100%

THE LT. COL. BILL KILGORE HYPOTHESIS

0000 HRS
0100 HRS
0200 HRS
0300 HRS
0400 HRS
0500 HRS
0600 HRS
0700 HRS
0800 HRS
0900 HRS
1000 HRS
1100 HRS
1200 HRS
1300 HRS
1400 HRS
1500 HRS
1600 HRS
1700 HRS
1800 HRS
1900 HRS
2000 HRS
2100 HRS
2200 HRS
2300 HRS

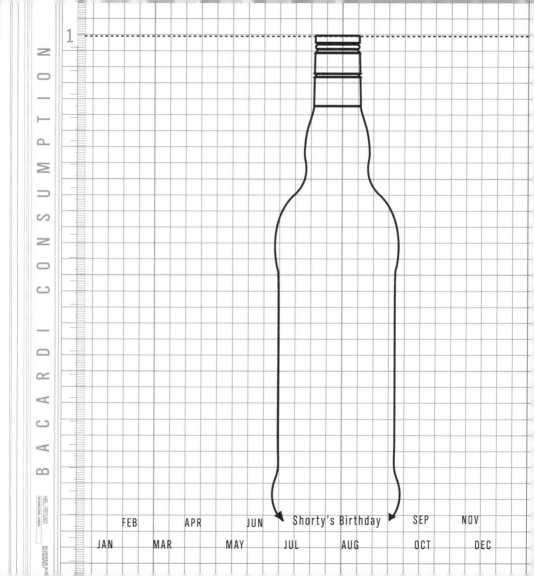

BACARDI CONSUMPTION

1

JAN FEB MAR APR MAY JUN JUL Shorty's Birthday AUG SEP OCT NOV DEC

FEAR   ANGER   HATE   SUFFERING   SO SIMPLE, IT IS
{ 1 }   { 2 }   { 3 }   { 4 }   { 5 }

5

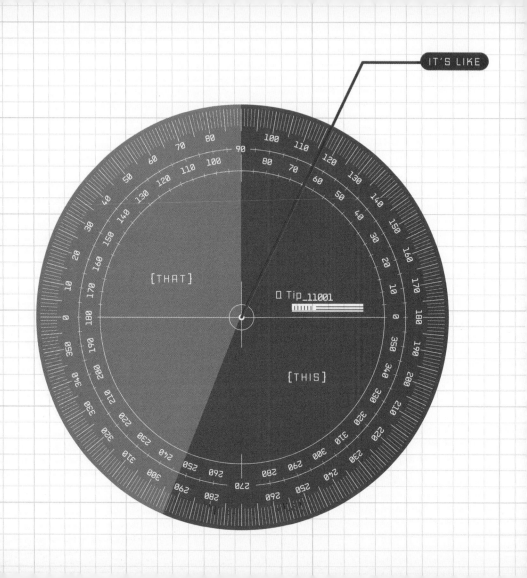

IT'S LIKE

[THAT]

Q Tip_11001

[THIS]

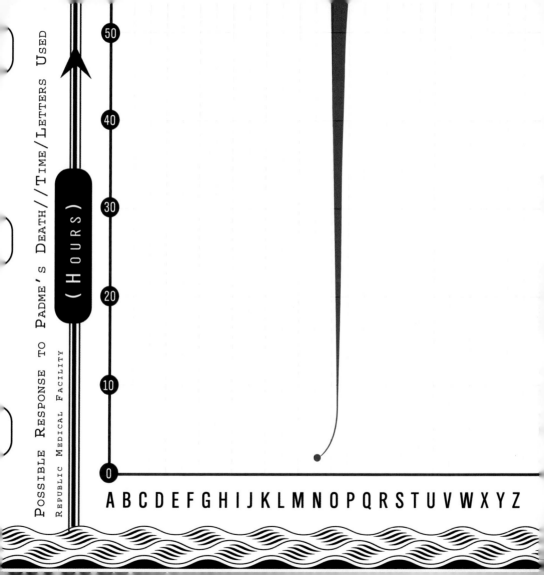

POSSIBLE RESPONSE TO PADME'S DEATH//TIME/LETTERS USED

REPUBLIC MEDICAL FACILITY

(HOURS)

50

40

30

20

10

0

A B C D E F G H I J K L M N O P Q R S T U V W X Y Z

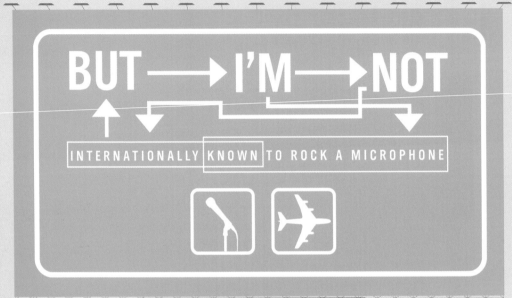

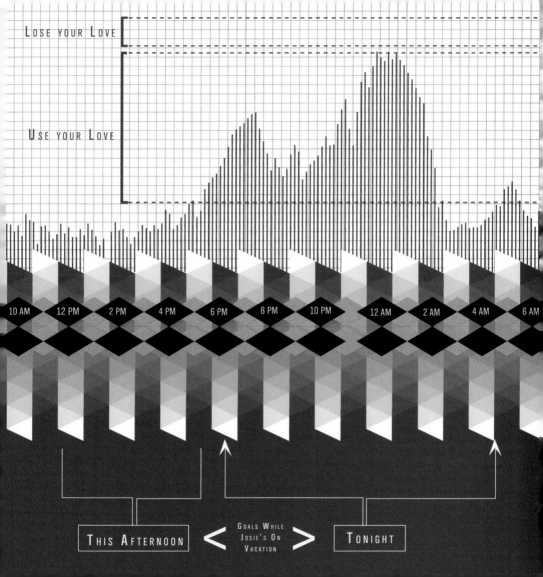

GEOGRAPHICAL REGIONS OF THE WORLD
FAVORED BY TOTOS OF POP-CULTURAL NOTE

CANINE (CIRCA 1939)
HUMAN (CIRCA 1982)

jenny 867-5307

Guest Check

Date	Table Number	Number in Party

I fell in love again ⟶ All things go; all things go

Drove to Chicago ⟶ All things know; all things know

We sold our clothes to the state ⟶ I don't mind; I don't mind

I made a lot of mistakes ⟶ In my mind; in my mind

⟶ All things grow; all things grow

You came to take us, to re-create us
We had our mindset
you had to find it

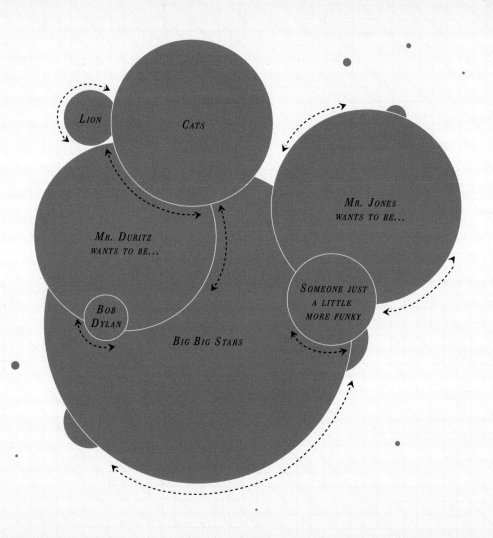

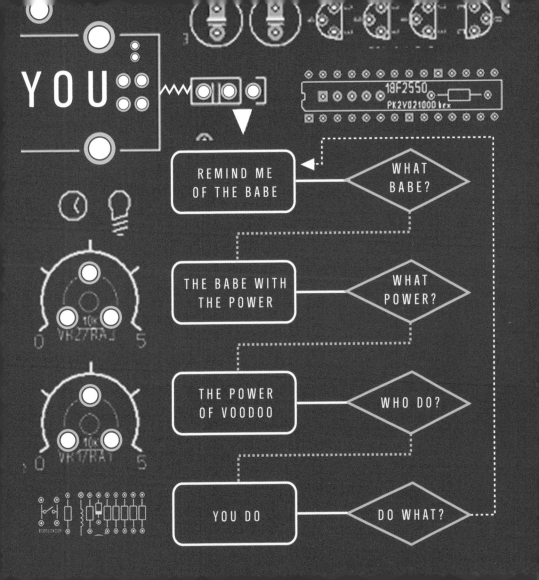

N

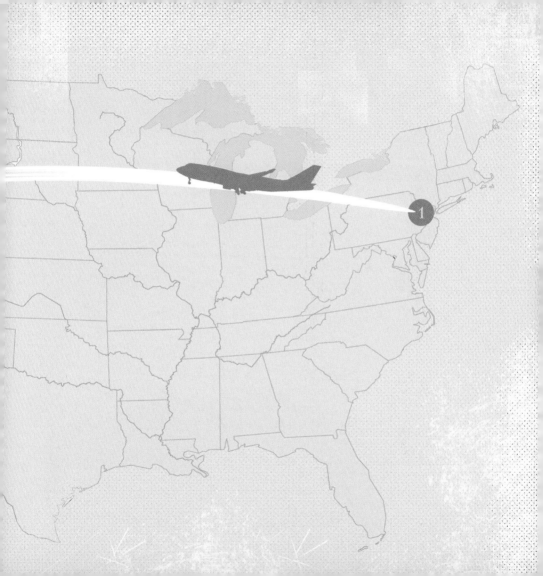

50 Cent : you :: fat kid

```
$me = new Person ("Rivers Cuomo")

$you = new Person

        ("Rivers Cuomo's Significant Other")



if ($you-)desire() == "destroy my sweater"){

        while($me-)walk()){

                $you-)action



                ("hold this string,""sweater")

        }

    }
```

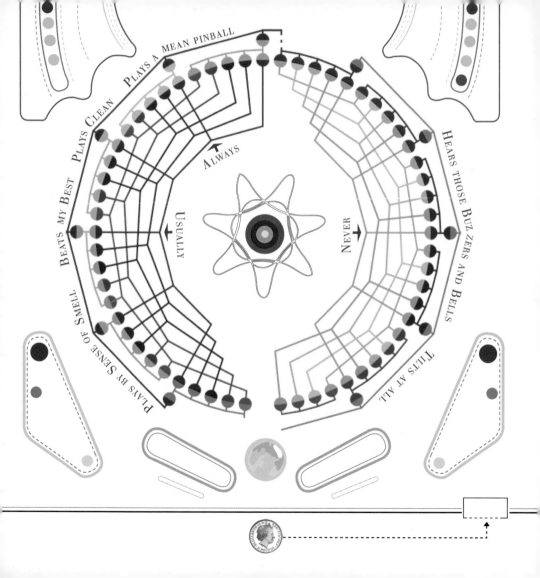

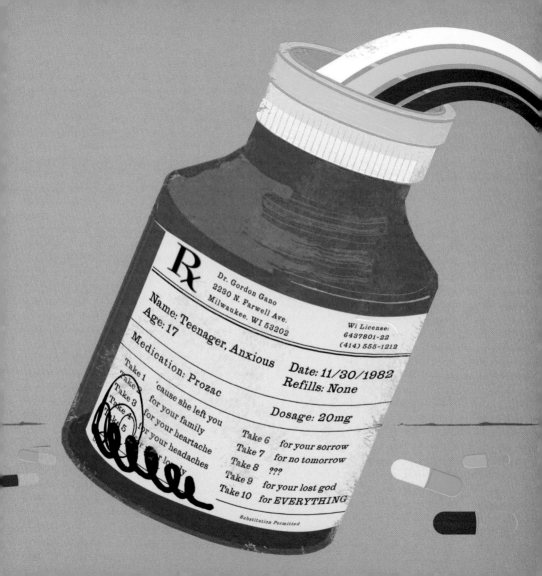

The Darkness

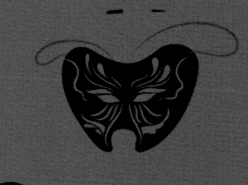

TOM CRUISE'S
SENSE OF METAPHYSICAL
WELL-BEING

{ PER THE DICTATES
OF STANLEY KUBRICK
CIRCA 1999 }

FRANKIE SAYS

WHEN YOU WANT
TO GO DO IT

↓

RELAX

(DON'T DO IT)

WHEN YOU WANT
TO SOCK IT TO IT

WHEN YOU WANT
TO COME

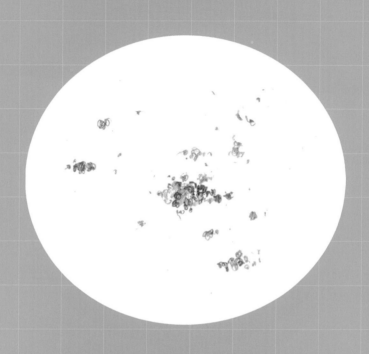

● AMOUNT OF PIE EATEN   ◍ AMOUNT OF PIE NOT YET EATEN

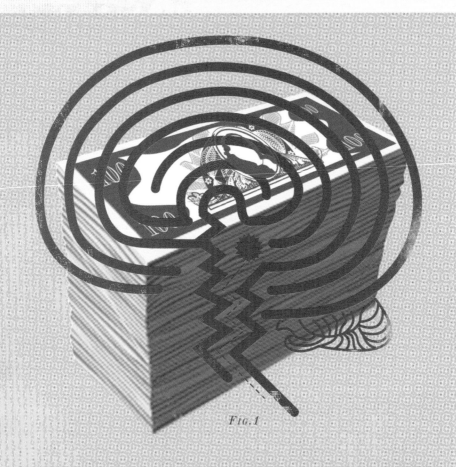

Fig.1

COGNITIVE EFFECTS OF ENDO, GIN, AND JUICE

Fɪɢ.2

{ Due to Smoking and Sipping on,
Respectively }

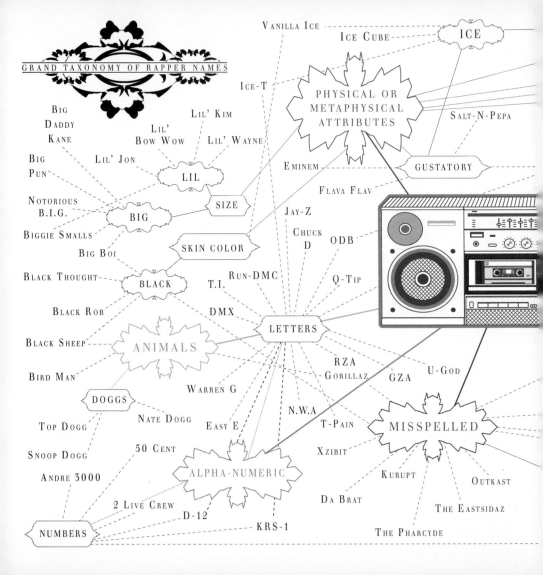

GRAND TAXONOMY OF RAPPER NAMES

VANILLA ICE

ICE CUBE

ICE

ICE-T

PHYSICAL OR METAPHYSICAL ATTRIBUTES

SALT-N-PEPA

BIG DADDY KANE

LIL' KIM

LIL' BOW WOW

LIL' WAYNE

LIL' JON

EMINEM

GUSTATORY

BIG PUN

LIL

FLAVA FLAV

SIZE

NOTORIOUS B.I.G.

BIG

JAY-Z

BIGGIE SMALLS

SKIN COLOR

CHUCK D

ODB

BIG BOI

BLACK THOUGHT

RUN-DMC

Q-TIP

T.I.

BLACK ROB

BLACK

DMX

BLACK SHEEP

ANIMALS

LETTERS

BIRD MAN

RZA

GORILLAZ

GZA

U-GOD

DOGGS

WARREN G

TOP DOGG

NATE DOGG

EASY E

N.W.A

MISSPELLED

SNOOP DOGG

50 CENT

T-PAIN

ANDRE 3000

XZIBIT

ALPHA-NUMERIC

KURUPT

OUTKAST

2 LIVE CREW

DA BRAT

THE EASTSIDAZ

D-12

NUMBERS

KRS-1

THE PHARCYDE

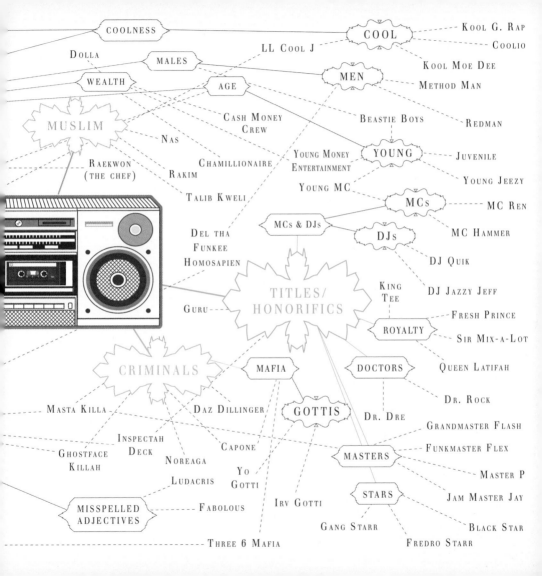

Page	Reference
5	"Bust a Move" Young MC 1989
6	"Should I Stay or Should I Go" The Clash 1982
7	*Trading Places* 1983
8	"Harder, Better, Faster, Stronger" Daft Punk 2001
9	"We Built This City" Starship 1985
10	"The Bad Touch" *The Bloodhound Gang* 1999
11	"Whip It" Devo 1980
13	*The Blues Brothers* 1980
14–15	"Friday I'm in Love" The Cure 1992
16	"Borderline" Madonna 1984
17	"...Baby One More Time" Britney Spears 1998
18	"Mrs. Robinson" Simon and Garfunkel 1968
19	*Coming to America* 1988
20	"Mo Money Mo Problems" The Notorious B.I.G. 1997

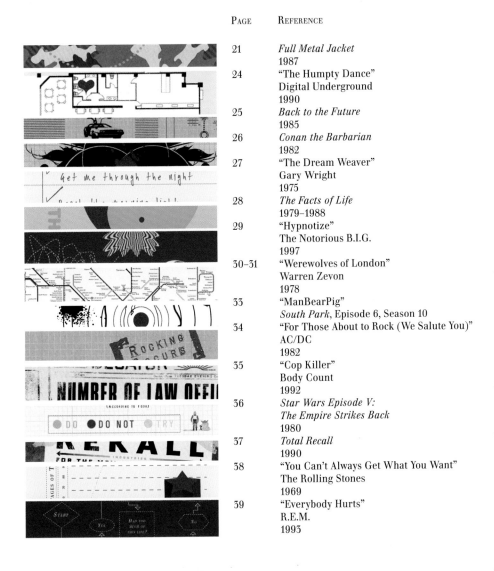

PAGE	REFERENCE
21	*Full Metal Jacket* 1987
24	"The Humpty Dance" Digital Underground 1990
25	*Back to the Future* 1985
26	*Conan the Barbarian* 1982
27	"The Dream Weaver" Gary Wright 1975
28	*The Facts of Life* 1979–1988
29	"Hypnotize" The Notorious B.I.G. 1997
30–31	"Werewolves of London" Warren Zevon 1978
33	"ManBearPig" *South Park*, Episode 6, Season 10
34	"For Those About to Rock (We Salute You)" AC/DC 1982
35	"Cop Killer" Body Count 1992
36	*Star Wars Episode V: The Empire Strikes Back* 1980
37	*Total Recall* 1990
38	"You Can't Always Get What You Want" The Rolling Stones 1969
39	"Everybody Hurts" R.E.M. 1993

PAGE	REFERENCE
40	"Hello Goodbye" The Beatles 1967
42	"One Way or Another" Blondie 1979
43	"O.P.P." Naughty by Nature 1991
44-45	"Rock and Roll All Nite" Kiss 1975
46	*The Sixth Sense* 1999
47	*I Know What You Did Last Summer* 1997
48	"When Doves Cry" Prince 1984
49	*RoboCop* 1987
51	"Rock You Like a Hurricane" The Scorpions 1984
52-53	*This Is Spinal Tap* 1984
54	*The Karate Kid* 1984
55	"Sunglasses at Night" Corey Hart 1983
56-57	*Top Gun* 1986
58	*Anchorman: The Legend of Ron Burgundy* 2004
59	"I'd Do Anything for Love (But I Won't Do That)" Meat Loaf 1993

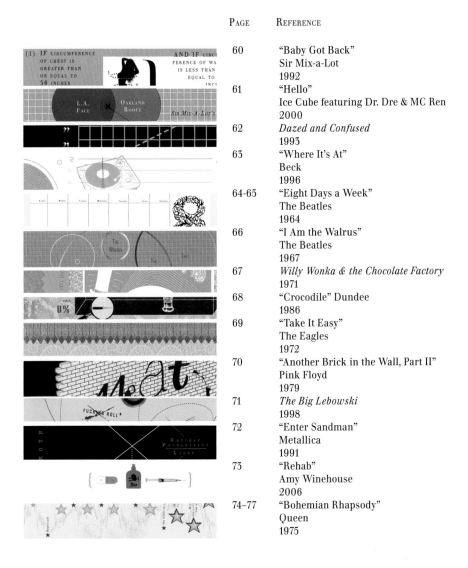

PAGE	REFERENCE
60	"Baby Got Back" Sir Mix-a-Lot 1992
61	"Hello" Ice Cube featuring Dr. Dre & MC Ren 2000
62	*Dazed and Confused* 1993
63	"Where It's At" Beck 1996
64-65	"Eight Days a Week" The Beatles 1964
66	"I Am the Walrus" The Beatles 1967
67	*Willy Wonka & the Chocolate Factory* 1971
68	"Crocodile" Dundee 1986
69	"Take It Easy" The Eagles 1972
70	"Another Brick in the Wall, Part II" Pink Floyd 1979
71	*The Big Lebowski* 1998
72	"Enter Sandman" Metallica 1991
73	"Rehab" Amy Winehouse 2006
74–77	"Bohemian Rhapsody" Queen 1975

PAGE	REFERENCE
78	"Sometimes a Pony Gets Depressed" Silver Jews 2005
80	"Two Out of Three Ain't Bad" Meat Loaf 1977
81	"Too Legit to Quit" MC Hammer 1991
82–83	"Don't Cry for Me Argentina" Madonna in *Evita* 1996
84	"Bitches Ain't Shit" Dr. Dre 1992
85	*Monty Python and the Holy Grail* 1975
86	"California Girls" The Beach Boys 1965
87	"Nuthin but a 'G' Thang" Dr. Dre featuring Snoop Dogg 1993
88–89	"Sucker M.C.'s (Krush Groove 1)" Run-D.M.C. 1984
90–91	"All My Ex's Live in Texas" George Strait 1987
92	"Get Down on It" Kool & The Gang 1981
93	*Napoleon Dynamite* 2004
94	"Brain Damage/ Eclipse" Pink Floyd 1973
95	*Spaceballs* 1987

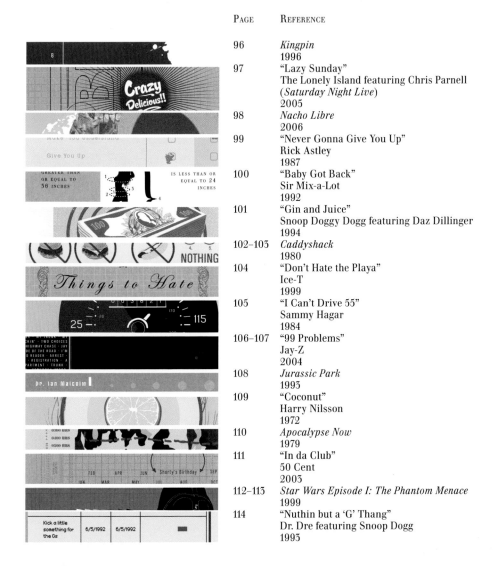

PAGE	REFERENCE
96	*Kingpin* 1996
97	"Lazy Sunday" The Lonely Island featuring Chris Parnell (*Saturday Night Live*) 2005
98	*Nacho Libre* 2006
99	"Never Gonna Give You Up" Rick Astley 1987
100	"Baby Got Back" Sir Mix-a-Lot 1992
101	"Gin and Juice" Snoop Doggy Dogg featuring Daz Dillinger 1994
102–103	*Caddyshack* 1980
104	"Don't Hate the Playa" Ice-T 1999
105	"I Can't Drive 55" Sammy Hagar 1984
106–107	"99 Problems" Jay-Z 2004
108	*Jurassic Park* 1993
109	"Coconut" Harry Nilsson 1972
110	*Apocalypse Now* 1979
111	"In da Club" 50 Cent 2003
112–113	*Star Wars Episode I: The Phantom Menace* 1999
114	"Nuthin but a 'G' Thang" Dr. Dre featuring Snoop Dogg 1993

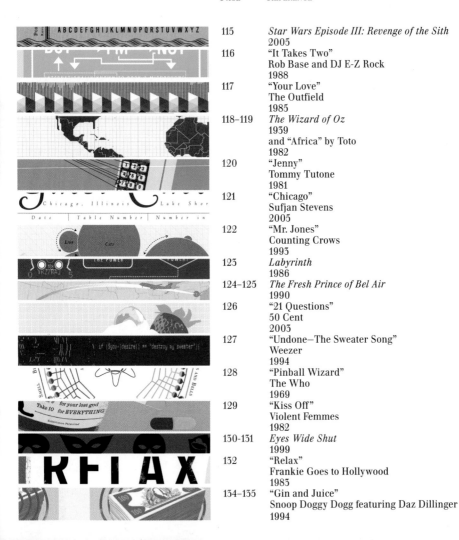

PAGE   REFERENCE

115   *Star Wars Episode III: Revenge of the Sith*
2005

116   "It Takes Two"
Rob Base and DJ E-Z Rock
1988

117   "Your Love"
The Outfield
1985

118–119   *The Wizard of Oz*
1939
and "Africa" by Toto
1982

120   "Jenny"
Tommy Tutone
1981

121   "Chicago"
Sufjan Stevens
2005

122   "Mr. Jones"
Counting Crows
1993

123   *Labyrinth*
1986

124–125   *The Fresh Prince of Bel Air*
1990

126   "21 Questions"
50 Cent
2003

127   "Undone—The Sweater Song"
Weezer
1994

128   "Pinball Wizard"
The Who
1969

129   "Kiss Off"
Violent Femmes
1982

130-131   *Eyes Wide Shut*
1999

132   "Relax"
Frankie Goes to Hollywood
1983

134–135   "Gin and Juice"
Snoop Doggy Dogg featuring Daz Dillinger
1994